MICHIG

JEOPARDY!

Answers and Questions About Our State

by
Carole Marsh

This activity book has material which correlates with Michigan's Social Studies Content Standards. At every opportunity, we have tried to relate information to the History and Social Science, English, Science, Math, Civics, Economics, and Computer Technology SSCS directives. For additional information, go to our websites: **www.michiganexperience.com** or **www.gallopade.com**.

Reading
Reference / Research
Reinforcement

Gallopade is proud to be a member of these educational organizations and associations:

SHOPA MEMBER™
School, Home, & Office Products Association

NSSEA

The MICHIGAN Experience Series

The Michigan Experience!

My First Pocket Guide to Michigan!

The Big Michigan Reproducible Activity Book

The Michigan Coloring Book!

My First Book About Michigan!

Michigan Jeopardy: Answers and Questions About Our State

Michigan Jography: A Fun Run Through Our State

The Michigan Experience! Sticker Pack

The Michigan Experience! Poster/Map

Discover Michigan CD-ROM

Michigan "GEO" Bingo Game

Michigan "HISTO" Bingo Game

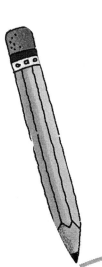

A Word... from the Author

The word is Jeopardy!

I'm sure you've all seen this popular game show. Actually, it's not much different from something kids seem to hate—the good, old-fashioned pop quiz! But how much more fun plain, boring questions and answers are when they're switcherooed into answers and questions!

I'm not trying to copy the actual Jeopardy game show format. I've just tried to use the reverse: "Here's the answer, now what's the question?" formula to make the facts about our state as interesting and intriguing as possible. Also, I think this format is a good double-check to see just how much all that history and geography is registering. Kids often know "facts" only in the memorized-order they learned them, which does not exactly = true knowledge, even if they do pass their tests.

The Answers and Questions on the next pages cover our state's history, geography, people, and much more. You can use the book in a variety of ways. If students want to read it on their own, they'll need to use a sheet of paper to cover the answers, oops!, I mean the questions. You could keep the book on the kitchen table and play Jeopardy while you eat breakfast. In the classroom, you could give the answers orally and let kids give the questions.

Whatever you do, keep score, have fun, let all ages participate, use wrong answers (I mean questions!) as the starting point for improved learning. Let kids have a chance to create their own Jeopardy answers and questions (it's much harder than it looks!). The only thing that should really be put in jeopardy are your frown muscles!

Carole Marsh

MICHIGAN Trivia

Answer: The Michigan state capital

QUESTION: What is Lansing?

Answer: The Michigan state motto

QUESTION: What is "If You Seek a Pleasant Peninsula, Look About You"?

Answer: The Michigan nickname

QUESTION: What is the Wolverine State?

Answer: The Michigan state soil

QUESTION: What is Kalkaska sand?

Answer: The Michigan state song

QUESTION: What is "Michigan, My Michigan?"

MICHIGAN
All Around Our State

Answer: The Upper and Lower Peninsulas of Michigan are separated by this body of water.

QUESTION: What are the Straits of Mackinac?

Answer: The Lower Peninsula borders these states to the south

QUESTION: What are Indiana and Ohio?

Answer: The highest point in Michigan

QUESTION: What is Mount Arvon?

Answer: State which borders the Upper Peninsula to the south.

QUESTION: What is Wisconsin?

Answer: Great Lake that does NOT touch Michigan

Hurry! I'm next.

QUESTION: What is Lake Ontario?

MICHIGAN
Forts

Answer: A fort established in 1701 by Antoine de la Mothe Cadillac which eventually became the city of Detroit.

QUESTION: What is Fort Pontchartrain?

Answer: Forts built by the French on Mackinac Island and at Mackinaw City to control the fur trade and that serve as museums today

QUESTION: What are Forts Mackinac and Michilimackinac?

Answer: The state's first amateur acting troupe was formed by officers here who performed *Rivals* and *The Mock Duke* beginning in 1798.

QUESTION: What is Fort Detroit?

Answer: Spanish forces captured this fort in 1781 and held it for one day before being driven out.

QUESTION: What is Fort St. Joseph?

Answer: The oldest surviving lighthouse on Lake Huron is at this fort

QUESTION: What is Fort Gratiot?

MICHIGAN
People

Answer: Around 97 percent of Michigan's population live on this peninsula.

QUESTION: What is the Lower Peninsula?

Answer: The largest Native American tribe in Michigan

QUESTION: Who are the Ojibwa, or Chippewa?

Answer: Three of the biggest ethnic groups found in Michigan today

QUESTION: What are German, Polish, and Irish?

Answer: The first mosque for this religious group in the U.S. was built in 1919 in Highland Park.

QUESTION: Who are Moslems?

Answer: The majority of this group of people came from the southern states to Michigan in the 1930s and 1940s

QUESTION: Who are African-Americans?

Answer: The first European explorers in Michigan were looking for this route to the Pacific Ocean when they came to Michigan.

QUESTION: What is a Northwest Passage?

Answer: First European to to visit the Upper Peninsula around 1620

QUESTION: Who was Étienne Brulé?

Answer: Jesuit missionary who established a mission at Keweenaw Bay in 1660

QUESTION: Who was René Ménard?

Answer: He founded Michigan's first permanent settlement, Sault Ste. Marie, in 1668.

QUESTION: Who was Father Jacques Marquette?

Answer: A name given to French-Canadian fur traders who paddled their canoes deep into Indian territory.

QUESTION: Who were voyageurs?

Answer: Ottawa chief and his warriors who kept Detroit under siege for almost seven months

QUESTION: Who was Pontiac?

Answer: Michigan was part of the area known as this in 1787 which included Ohio, Indiana, Illinois, Wisconsin, and parts of Minnesota.

QUESTION: What is the Northwest Territory?

Answer: Michigan was included in this new territory created by Congress in 1800.

QUESTION: What is the Indiana Territory?

Answer: Conflict that erupted between the U.S. and England in 1812

QUESTION: What was the War of 1812?

Answer: Michigan writer and educator in the 1800s who wrote about the Native Americans' way of life and preserved their legends

QUESTION: Who was Henry Rowe Schoolcraft?

Good Ol' USA!

Answer: This allows freighters passage between Lake Huron and Lake Superior.

QUESTION: What are the Soo Locks?

Answer: Desert-like expanse of sand dunes near Empire, the largest of which was in the shape of a bear

QUESTION: What is the Sleeping Bear Dunes National Lakeshore?

Answer: The longest river in Michigan

QUESTION: What is the Grand River?

Answer: The largest freshwater lake in the world

QUESTION: What is Lake Superior?

Answer: The 363-mile (584-kilometer) waterway that connects the Great Lakes to the Atlantic Ocean opened in 1825.

QUESTION: What is the Erie Canal?

Water, water everywhere!

MICHIGAN
Real Estate

It's great to be home again.

Yeah!

Answer: One of the largest copper mines in the world in the 1800s and today, visitors can descend one mile or more to explore the caverns.

QUESTION: What is the Arcadian Mine?

Answer: Made up of 200 tiny islets, it is Michigan's only national park and is home to America'a largest herd of moose and a pack of wolves.

QUESTION: What is Isle Royale?

Answer: City known as the "Cherry Capital of the World?

QUESTION: What is Traverse City?

Answer: City that is the hometown to Gerald R. Ford, the 38th U.S. president

QUESTION: What is Grand Rapids?

Answer: City that is home to the University of Michigan

QUESTION: What is Ann Arbor?

Howdy neighbors!

MICHIGAN
Slavery and the Cival War

Answer: Secret network that helped escaped slaves get to the North

QUESTION: What is the Underground Railroad?

Answer: People who were against slavery

QUESTION: Who were abolitionists?

Answer: Political party founded in Michigan in 1854 around the banner of antislavery

QUESTION: What is the Republican Party?

Answer: Michigan woman who disguised herself as a man and fought with Union forces

QUESTION: Who was Sarah Emma Edmonds?

Answer: A Michigan regiment that captured Jefferson Davis in Georgia after the Southern armies collapsed

QUESTION: What was the 4th Michigan Calvary?

MICHIGAN

Education

Answer: Judge who came up with the first plan for an extensive public education program in 1817

QUESTION: Who was Judge Augustus Woodward?

Answer: Because of the 1874 Kalamazoo Case decided by the state supreme court, Michigan was the first state to include these in its school systems.

QUESTION: What are high schools?

Answer: Founded in 1855, this was the first public college in America to offer agricultural courses for credit.

QUESTION: What is Michigan State University?

Answer: It was established in 1849 in Ypsilanti as the first state teachers' college west of New York.

QUESTION: What is Eastern Michigan University?

Answer: This Michigan State University campus is the largest in the state's university system

QUESTION: What is East Lansing?

MICHIGAN Indians

Answer: The Chippewa (Ojibwa), Ottowa, and Potawatomi were the main tribes in Michigan and were members of this confederation.

QUESTION: What was the Three Fires Confederation?

Answer: Chippewa chief who led the massacre of Fort Michilimackinac on June 2, 1763

QUESTION: Who was Minavavana?

Answer: In the mid-1800s, 30 chiefs from different tribes met at Greensky Hill and each planted a tree and vowed to live in peace as long as the tree grew.

QUESTION: What was the Council Trees of the Ottawa?

Answer: Known as the "Snowshoe Priest," he was a teacher, priest, and legal advisor to Michigan's Indians

QUESTION: Who was Father Frederic Barga?

Answer: This Potawatomi chief was poisoned by his people after selling their tribal land for $10,000 and trying to get them to move to Kansas.

QUESTION: Who was Chief Sawauquette?

Women Who Were First

Answer: She founded the Detroit Parliamentary Law Club and was nominated for president in 1940 during a mock Republican Convention held by women.

QUESTION: Who was Emma Augusta Stowell Fox?

Answer: She was the first woman to command a U.S. Army Recruiting Armed Forces Examining and Entrance Station.

QUESTION: Who was Lieutenant Colonel Mattie V. Parker?

Answer: She created the Women's Auxiliary Ferrying Squadron during World War II, which later became the Women's Air Force Service Pilots (WASPS).

QUESTION: Who was Nancy Harkness Love?

Answer: She was the first Michigan woman elected to Congress and was the first female member of the House Judiciary Committee.

QUESTION: Who was Ruth Thompson?

Answer: She was the first African-American woman to be on the cover of *Time* magazine, and the first female inducted into the Rock and Roll Hall of Fame.

QUESTION: Who is Aretha Franklin?

Ready for your 15 minutes?

Yeah!

MICHIGAN
Government

Answer: Number of counties in Michigan

QUESTION: What is 83?

Answer: Branch of government that carries out the state's laws

QUESTION: What is the executive branch?

Answer: Branch of state government that makes the state's laws

QUESTION: What is the legislative branch?

Answer: The branch of state government that interprets the laws

QUESTION: What is the judicial branch?

Answer: Michigander who became the first U.S. president not voted into office

QUESTION: Who is Gerald R. Ford?

MICHIGAN
Lost in the Lakes

Hey Skipper!

Answer: Whitefish Point is the end of this 80-mile stretch where 300 shipwrecks have been recorded.

QUESTION: What was the Graveyard of the Great Lakes?

Answer: Coast Guard ship based in Cheboygan which breaks up ice floes that would block shipping lanes

QUESTION: What is the *Mackinaw?*

Answer: Ship that sank in Lake Superior in the Graveyard of the Great Lakes in 1975

QUESTION: What was the *Edmund Fitzgerald?*

Answer: Ship that sank near the Detroit River in Lake Erie with a cargo of locomotives

QUESTION: What was the *Clairion?*

What did you call me?

Answer: Ship lost in 1846 that sank with a cargo of kegged whiskey

QUESTION: What was the *Lexington?*

MICHIGAN
State Symbols

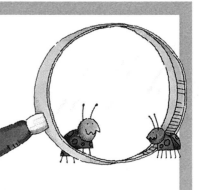

Answer: The state bird

QUESTION: What is the robin?

Answer: Apple blossom

QUESTION: What is the state flower?

Answer: The state fish

QUESTION: What is the brook trout?

Answer: The state stone

QUESTION: What is the Petoskey stone?

Answer: The state gem

QUESTION: What is the Isle Royale greenstone?

MICHIGAN
Motown

Answer: He borrowed $800 from his parents and set up a small recording studio on Grand Boulevard in Detroit which became Motown.

QUESTION: Who is Berry Gordy, Jr.?

Answer: He was the lead singer of the Miracles and also a Motown vice-president.

QUESTION: Who was Smokey Robinson?

Answer: Motown moved its operation to this city in 1972.

QUESTION: What is Los Angeles?

Answer: She wrote and performed Motown's first number-one hit.

QUESTION: Who was Mary Wells?

Answer: Girl group who began as backup singers and had 15 consecutive hits in 10 years

QUESTION: Who were the Supremes?

MICHIGAN
The Fine Arts

Answer: This Mexican painter's murals of the working world of the automotive industry are shown at the Detroit Institute of Arts.

QUESTION: Who is Diego Rivera?

Answer: The largest community theater in Michigan

QUESTION: What is the Grand Rapids Civic Theater?

Answer: Considered the "Father of Rock and Roll", this Highland Park musician's record "Rock Around the Clock" topped the charts in 1955

QUESTION: Who is Bill Haley?

Answer: The author of *Big Two-Hearted River,* whose hero was fishing at Seney in the Upper Peninsula

QUESTION: Who was Ernest Hemingway?

Answer: Linda Hunt and Meredith Baxter are among the graduates of this arts academy for students in grades 9-12.

QUESTION: What is the Interlochen Arts Academy?

MICHIGAN Sports

Answer: With 20 world championship courses and 10 golf resorts, the north central coast has earned this nickname.

QUESTION: What is "America's Summer Golf Capital"?

Answer: City that hosts the Crim 10-mile Run in the fall which draws runners from all over the world

QUESTION: What is Flint?

Answer: This baseball team was a charter member of the American League in 1901.

QUESTION: What are the Detroit Tigers (formerly the Detroit Wolverines)?

Answer: Professional team that makes its home at the Pontiac Silverdome

QUESTION: What are the Detroit Lions?

Answer: The Joe Louis Arena is home to this team which won the Stanley Cup in 1997.

QUESTION: What are the Detroit Red Wings?

MICHIGAN
State Stuff

Answer: It comes from the Ojibwa (Chippewa) word *michigama* which means "great water"

QUESTION: Where does the name Michigan come from?

Answer: The state tree

QUESTION: What is the white pine?

Answer: The state reptile

QUESTION: What is the painted turtle?

Answer: The bridge that connects the two halves of Michigan across the Straits of Mackinac

QUESTION: What is Mackinac Bridge?

Answer: This bridge that connects Detroit, Michigan and Windsor, Ontario was the first to connect two countries

QUESTION: What is the Ambassador Bridge?

MICHIGAN
The Economy

Answer: Henry Ford developed this to speed up the production of automobiles.

QUESTION: What is an assembly line?

Answer: Mining for this mineral began in 1845 and ended in 1969.

QUESTION: What is copper?

Answer: Michigan produces 20 percent of the nation's output of this mineral.

QUESTION: What is iron ore?

Answer: It is making a comeback, and 4 million Christmas trees harvested in Michigan each year prove this.

QUESTION: What is the timber industry?

Answer: These crops total almost 62 percent of Michigan's farm income.

QUESTION: What are corn, hay, and soybeans?

MICHIGAN
Statehood

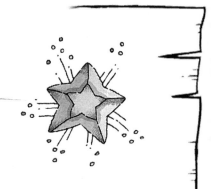

Answer: January 26, 1837

QUESTION: When did Michigan become a state?

Answer: Michigan was admitted to the U.S. as this state.

QUESTION: What is 26th?

Answer: A dispute over this small strip of land with Ohio delayed Michigan's statehood.

QUESTION: What was the Toledo Strip?

Answer: To settle the dispute, Ohio was given the Toledo Strip and Michigan was given this area.

QUESTION: What is the Upper Peninsula?

Answer: He was elected as the first governor of Michigan.

QUESTION: Who was Stevens T. Mason?

MICHIGAN
Automobiles

Answer: He built the first inexpensive automobile in 1890.

QUESTION: Who was Ransom Olds?

Answer: He created the Model T.

QUESTION: Who was Henry Ford?

Answer: Ford, General Motors, and Chrysler all have headquarters in this Michigan city.

QUESTION: What is Detroit?

Answer: The first self-propelled vehicle was a steam-powered automobile built in the winter of 1884-85 by these brothers in Memphis.

QUESTION: Who were John and Thomas Clegg?

Answer: Known as the "Godfather of the Automobile Industry"

QUESTION: Who was William Crapo Durant?

MICHIGAN
Food Barons

Answer: He was experimenting with a new wheat bread recipe when he produced the first corn flakes.

QUESTION: Who was W.K. Kellogg?

Answer: City known as the "Cereal Capital of the World"

QUESTION: What is Battle Creek?

Answer: When the Kelloggs refused to go into partnership with him, he developed his own cereal and sold it door-to-door.

QUESTION: Who was C.W. Post?

Answer: All she got for inventing Stove Top Stuffing for General Foods was a $125 bonus and a plaque.

QUESTION: Who is Ruth Siems?

Answer: Impatient because his wife took so long making baby food by forcing vegetables through a strainer, he developed a method to make canned baby food at his father's cannery in Fremont.

QUESTION: Who was Dan Gerber?

MICHIGAN
Fairs and Festivals

Answer: Ice-fishing festival that takes place in Houghton Lake in January

QUESTION: What is Tip-Up Town, USA?

Answer: The Grand Prix is held in this city in June.

QUESTION: What is Detroit?

Answer: The Upper Peninsula State Fair is held here in mid-August.

QUESTION: What is Escanaba?

Answer: Greenfield Village in this city includes Henry Ford's birthplace and Thomas Edison's Menlo Park laboratory.

QUESTION: What is Dearborn?

Answer: City that hosts a 10-day Michigan Festival each year featuring artists, craftworkers, and performers from throughout the state

QUESTION: What is Lansing?

MICHIGAN
Cities and Towns

Answer: The largest town in the Upper Peninsula sits on a high cliff overlooking Lake Superior.

QUESTION: What is Marquette?

Answer: This city started as a fur-trading outpost and is now center of the sugar beet industry.

QUESTION: What is Saginaw?

Answer: Home of the Labor Museum, the only museum dedicated to the history of working men and women

QUESTION: What is Flint?

Answer: Names considered for this city in 1847 included Michigan, Pewanogowink, Swedenborg, and El Dorado

QUESTION: What is Lansing?

Answer: Incorporated in 1815, this city was Michigan's capital for a while before Lansing was chosen.

QUESTION: What is Detroit?

MICHIGAN
Labor

Answer: Many of these organizations formed to speak out for the workers.

QUESTION: What are labor unions?

Answer: Farmers joined this organization, similar to the unions, to help them over the rough spots.

QUESTION: What is the Grange?

Answer: The Knights of Labor got their supporters elected to office and in 1883 the legislature formed this to help laborers.

QUESTION: What is the Michigan Department of Labor?

Answer: Group that led labor stoppages in the 1920s and 1930s in the automobile industry

QUESTION: What is the United Auto Workers?

Answer: More than 150,000 workers gathered on Detroit's Cadillac Square in February 1937 to support workers striking at this automobile company.

QUESTION: What is Chrysler?

MICHIGAN
African-Americans

Answer: He laid the groundwork for the United Nations in 1944 and was the first African-American to receive the Nobel Peace Prize.

QUESTION: Who was Ralph Bunche?

Answer: Born Malcolm Little, he was raised in Lansing and formed the Organization for Afro-American Unity.

QUESTION: Who was Malcolm X?

Answer: A member of the famed Tuskegee Airmen, he was elected as the first African-American mayor of Detroit in 1973 and served five terms.

QUESTION; Who is Coleman Young?

Answer: An abolitionist and supporter of women's rights, this former slave lived in Battle Creek.

QUESTION: Who was Sojourner Truth?

Answer: In 1963, he led 125,000 in a Detroit rally urging a nonviolent end to racial discrimination.

QUESTION: Who was Martin Luther King, Jr.?

MICHIGAN
Weather

Answer: They insulate the Lower Peninsula from very cold weather.

QUESTION: What are the Great Lakes?

Answer: Snowfall is heaviest here.

QUESTION: What is the Upper Peninsula?

Answer: 26 inches to 36 inches

QUESTION: What is the average annual precipitation?

Answer: Winds off these Great Lakes are the cause of heavy snow accumulations in areas close by.

QUESTION: What are Lakes Michigan and Superior?

Answer: Michigan has an average of 16 of these deadly windstorms each year.

QUESTION: What are tornadoes?

MICHIGAN

Potpourri

Answer: The first mile of this in the U.S. opened in 1909 in Wayne County.

QUESTION: What is paved highway?

Answer: Detroit police officer who came up with the idea of rigging an electric light system at intersections to help with traffic

QUESTION: Who was William L. Potts?

Answer: It covers 37 acres (15 hectares), weighs 1,000 tons (910 metric tons), is located on the Wisconsin-Michigan border and is sprouting a plague of mushrooms.

QUESTION: What is the "humongus fungus"?

Answer: It is the second-largest waterfall east of the Mississippi River, and Henry Wadsworth Longfellow wrote of its beauty in "Song of Hiawatha."

QUESTION: What is Upper Tahquamenon Falls?

Answer: It can be seen in front of the Uniroyal factory in Dearborn.

QUESTION: What is the "World's Largest Tire"?